Light From The West Window

Susan Phillips

Susan Phillips

The Mountain Ash Poetry Series introduces readers to emerging Alberta writers.

Editor: Jannie Edwards
Cover design: John Luckhurst
Cover art: Randolf Parker, *Moment of Light*
Interior design: Erin Creasey
Printed by: Priority Printing

Rowan Books gratefully acknowledges the support of the Canada Council and the Alberta Foundation for the Arts for our publishing program.

THE CANADA COUNCIL | LE CONSEIL DES ARTS
FOR THE ARTS | DU CANADA
SINCE 1957 | DEPUIS 1957

The Alberta
Foundation
for the Arts

Canadian Cataloguing in Publication Data

Phillips, Susan (Susan Elaine), 1953–
  Light from the west window

  Poems.
  ISBN 0-9685257-7-6

I. Title.
PS8581.H578L53 2001   C811'.6   C2001-911097-9
PR9199.4.P56L53 2001

Published in Canada by Rowan Books
410-10113-104 Street
Edmonton, Alberta
T5J 1A1
(780) 421-1544

for
Tom, Rachel and Blair

Table of Contents ❧

The Last Dress Up Summer ❧

"In June and gentle oven
Summer kingdoms simmer
As they come
And flower and leaf and love
Release
Their sweetest juice."

Anne Wilkinson
(In *June and Gentle Oven*)

Beyond The Back Gate

Past the horizon, past miles
of August beyond the back gate.
Like Columbus we worried
about falling off

steep red cliffs into the angry
South Saskatchewan River
flowing fast and muddy, down
to Medicine Hat.

The boys were always first
to spot the puff
of cloud moving quickly through
finger-combed skies, dragging

a wisp of cord tied
to an earthbound engine.
A gathering of speed,
our whoopsof recognition

and tall grasshopper leaps
over tangles of sun
burnt grass. We watched
for gophers

who scurried down holes, dug
to catch our ankles, wary
of the slip of cow patties
and rattlers

that sizzled and shook angry
reptile fists, slithered away
before we could uncoil.

The bounce of pennies
in pockets. The jangle of 'Race
to the tracks! Race
to the tracks!' The rush

of setting of copper lines before
the first blast
of engine whistle. A face
through the engine window

and the running away
and aways back,
before the train thundered
past and left us

with heroic medals,
jagged and flat. Now safe
in my sewing basket, those summers
beyond the back gate.

The Song I Hear

Sometimes, late at night my Grandmother sang
her hearing-aid turned off, she would

'Walk In The Garden Alone,' her voice a tremble
above the tumble of water filling the kitchen sink,
above the chatter-sleep of my sister curled
beside me on the Winnipeg couch, lost
in pony dreams. Grandmother filled the dark

with 'All Things Bright and Beautiful,'
the jubilant romp of braver notes
that skittered and slid over and under
musical bars, rebounded off tulip
papered walls. Only her joy was in tune.

Bassnote dinner plates, stainless steel
sopranos, curt cutlery chimes and
'All Things Wise And Wonderful' were returned
to drawers, one syllable at a time. As pots and pans
rumbled deep applause in Sunlight waters.

Her heather tones of Aberdeen mauve
imbued 'How Great Thou Art' with a pensive
tempo of ascending scale, lifting high
above sunburnt Alberta fields, beyond
the tangle of wind and dirt.

'And He Walked With Me' dried the last of the wet
from the orange Tupperware rack. '... and the joy we share'
was a swish across countertops and a thug
of cupboard doors. Lights turned off,
her hearing-aid returned, she recessed

down the hall on a hum of 'Peace in The Valley'
into hot summer nights
and '...the Power and Glory forever'
Amen.

Grandad Was One of The Players

I still smell the Players smoke
drifting up, through the open window,
from their room below. Through
the chilled dawn scent of still dust
and fresh dew, his smoke
swirling around my bed.

It's putrid breath retelling stories
of predictable sequence. A string
of deep staggered coughs
that played him out. Hold my breath,
hold my breath, believing
in my small sacrifice. "Breathe Grandad,
breathe."

I see him sitting on the edge
of his bed, puffs of white
wirey hair escaping the rim of his
sleeveless vest. Copper stained fingers
of his right hand holding the smoke.
I knew even then, it would kill him.
Grade five health class held no suprise.

I could hear his death in every breath,
smell it in his stale kisses see it
in the rotted corn kernel teeth
and the food he pushed aside.
There were small holes in his pants
where the ash missed the ground.

I miss my Grandfather,
a man of gentle love and fierce habit.
I still hold my breath
when I hear that familiar cough.

The Last Dress Up Summer

#1

Yesterday, I bought a full-length, black satin slip.
The one in the window of La Vie En Rose.
It reminded me of Lindy, of the last summer
of dress-up and pretend, of shiny silk blouses
and red-spike heels with metal-scuffed toes. Remnants
of what her mother left behind.

Lindy lived by the Catholic Church, in a house
of Christian charity encased
in pitted windows and pierced mesh
screens. Built for those in need, needing
their confessions every Sunday, eight AM.

I visited Lindy after lunch, after
my Grandmother lay down and her father left
for the Brick Plant. Paul McCartney
mellowed our growing senses as we shared
her chores, whispered secrets, ignored
the smells of Baby John. His diapers
to be washed Ivory new. While he rested in his crib

we entered her Mother's room, ruby and velvet.
Borrowed dreams of glamour as we strutted
before a foggy floor length mirror
at the end of the bed. Chests
high, hips swaying, our fingers
supported imaginary menthol filters,
imitating Rita the redhead
hostess at The High Top Grill.

Early that summer we learned not to touch
her mother's makeup, her perfume
still strong enough for Lindy's Dad to remember
to prevent Lindy from seeing me
until his four day drunk had passed.

Eight days for her bruises to fade.
Dressed in a black satin slip, we never noticed
the ring of stained armpits, greasy spot
under the left breast or the green
cotton stitches on the back. The black
satin slip that drooped to my waist,
stretching tight over my thighs. We were
glamour blind to skinny, scabby knees
and sunburnt arms until
Baby John's hunger marked the afternoons spent.

#2

Those afternoons Lindy taught me how to tease
and tousle my straight brown hair. I brushed
her long blonde curls, formed waves
as we talked of downtown
Calgary, the Chinook Mall,
the new drive-through window at A&W.
She talked about Gary of the dark

eyes, tight jeans and the anchor tattoo
on his right wrist, though he never left
Medicine Hat. He always kissed her
with jaws grinding, devouring
her tiny rose mouth. His eyes

were always open, watching me, watching
them, doing what I could never
tell my mother, Lindy dare not tell
her father and the car grease always
on Gary's fingers.

We said we would be friends forever
and write every week
or so.

#3

That Thanksgiving, I heard Grandma tell Mom,
Lindy's father was in jail. Baby John
was in foster care in the 'Hat and Lindy
was gone. I remember

murky pool of gravy between clumps
of mashed potatoes splattered against garlands
of lavender blooms circling my Sunday dinner plate.

I remembered Lindy yesterday,
when I bought a full length
black satin slip at La Vie En Rose.

Lori

Her name was Lori. Lasso scripted 'L,'
martini olive 'o,' swirl topped 'r,'
and full telescopic circle over 'i.'

A hollow that burned through the page,
allowing her to see beyond the red

checkerboard floors, trod with white polished
cowboy boots supporting bare
legs, a fringed denim skirt on naked
thighs. A gingham shirt artfully unbuttoned.

The circle over 'i,' her view beyond

beer glass kisses, tasting
of Sunday morning disappointment,
lacquered smoke-stenched hair styles,
token tips and grating girlie names
served up

in Rawhide Bill's Country Saloon.
Where hollow oh's were the response
to the Daily Specials she chalked
in pastel on a pine plank by the bar

in schoolgirl script, straight and solid
filled dots above the 'i' and 'j', closed type
for paying customers.

Only a telescopic circle
above the 'i' in her name,
an open window
for Lori.

Mr. Barrett

I watched him fall. The old man
from condo five, with the wild white hair
and hearing-aide squeal, who shuffled
across the lawn every morning
for 10 a.m. coffee. Only had 1/2 a cup,
said it kept him awake as he poured
in four packets of sugar. I watched him

fall. Not in a Hollywood crumple, he fell
head forward upon the lawn. I heard
the coconut thud, saw the twisted stretch
of him. I watched

his bent hand open and close,
taking and letting go,
as I stood stroke still, waiting
for the reruns, not knowing what to do.
I watched

the Adam's girl in the yellow bikini
kneel quietly beside him,
cover him with her towel, whisper
"Help's coming Mr Barrett, be still."
as she stroked his head. I watched

knowing, I could have done that,
I could have done
that.

Telling Tales

I tell them "Saturday mornings I need
a jog, a coffee and The Globe and Mail"
tell them "watch TV kids, I won't be long."

> Don't tell them I first saw his shadow
> through the General Store window, sitting
> behind the woodstove. His oversized hands
> cradling a crockery mug, his flat fingers
> flipping lids off Dairyland cream cups
> for the torn-eared tabby with a pink tongue
> that licked and licked them clean, rubbed
> in and around his legs as his hands stroked her fur.

I tell them "Daddy called last night, says
he loves us all."

> Don't tell them about his dark
> tangled curls, pierced left ear, stubbled chin
> or the medley of sleep robbed voices, a mumble
> of "Morning Josh" as they fill travel mugs, listen
> for car horns that drag them away to the mill,
> the cannery, the fishingboats. His gaze still
> on the horizon outside the salt etched window
> and once on me. A quick look, unable to see
> past my ten extra pounds.

I tell them "Daddy says it's hot in Calgary
and we need a trip to the Saan for new flip-flops
and sunhats and let's have burgers at the drive-in tonight."

> Don't tell them I saw him across the street
> under the faded awning of The Whaler's Pub.
> Saw a woman kiss his neck, her tongue
> in his ear. His clumsy fingers smoothed her
> sunbottled hair, made her look delicate,
> sleek as a cat in a leopard print top. His gaze
> grazed me in dim recognition, his wink

and the heat of the parking lot, the ketchup stain
on my shirt and the children's neon sunglasses.

I tell them "hurry, finish up, it's a night for ice cream
at The Scoop." Tell them "I think August is too hot
for coffee and jogs and let's call Daddy tonight."

Don't tell them the cottage windows will never
be clean enough or the bedsheets fresh enough,
the curtains will never press straight and the stains
behind the stove will never clean white, from the splash
of smashed blackberries I boil into jam and the jars
and jars of his shadow that I can't shake.

I tell them "On Friday we'll pack the car,
close up the cottage and finish summer
at home." Don't tell, don't tell, don't tell.

On The Vine

I covered my patio tomatoes tonight,
my prairie August fears, of early autumn frost.
Tucked them carefully under a bedsheet,
with bamboo stakes, holding a dome
above their green heads,

> 118 sailors in a submarine,
> 300 metres below the Barents Sea.
> attached to a Kursk vine

and watched night rain patter
and tumble off.

> feeling the chill of military duty.

I thought of the corded vine
that holds tomatoes close and taut,
nourishes them to fullness. The sun.
The earth, the water.

> "I was always pleased my son
> was on the Kursk, not drafted
> to Chechnya."

Thought of the brush of their velvet leaves
staining my fingers with fresh peatty scent.

> A young Russian wife,
> pregnant, waits
> and waits to hear
> "The British are coming,"
> as CNN feeds appetites
> and American subs circle.

A peck of magpies pace the roof
wait to slip past my notice.
A flurry of storm lifts the sheet,
I rush to adjust.

A smash of underwater currents,
on the prostrate ship, on the ocean floor
as the men listen for taps on the hull,
watch the dark through portholes
and wait.

Autumn Too Early ❧

> "Late afternoon, the light is waiting
> with the patience a body knows
> when it is just beginning
> to understand time."

Lorna Crozier
("Late Afternoon," from *A Saving Grace*)

Corn Fest in Kin Coulee

We dance light as moths over summer
cabbages, blurred by steamy vats
of earthy hue. Young fingers burn
to be first to reach for gold cobs
and speak with butter coated tongues.

We dance to Ian Tyson
"Weather's good there in the Fall" *
while old ones remember
years of drought, dust
darkened windows
and canning jars filled
with prairie weeds.

This year young girls gather
bouquets of garden greens
and colored blooms, offer them
to a blushing Corn Fest Queen.
Young Sally dreamed it would be her
one day, dressed in cream
and buttercup. Today

we dance golden
under swaying poplars
in Kin Coulee.

* Four Strong Winds

Amazed

Amaze, a maze:

a field of maize
with stalks so tall that small
children lose their way,
become lost. Their cries forever
frozen in ears

of Mothers amazed
they didn't know
which direction to follow
in the green and twisted light.

Like the maze,
the folly built at Hampton Court
with hedges so tall Henry could hide,
seduce the next conquest whose eyes,
bosom and chin would inspire
a revolution called amazing.

One man's appetite for fresh,
sweet and green. The tangled
weave of new paths cut in
a political labyrinth.

His need to plant
his randy seed, forever frozen
in the harvest cries of new
doctrines, a new church.

Autumn Too Early

It's too early for Autumn.
Summer still remembers her fields
half grown with tightfisted green,
late hollyhock bloom.

Through the west window, a garden swing:
a gleam of red molded seat, a spark
of silver chain, twisting

in a tangled dance that beckons, one
more ride above branches, one more
view above edging shadows, above
the sneaker-scuffed earth.
Before the rush

of five leaves, hidden
in the carragana hedge, entice all
to don crimson cloaks.

Return To School

1. Grey

The color of a seven a.m. sky.
Rain that spills and stains
the asphalt, greys the highway
Calgary to Edmonton.

The pass of metal wipers
across my windshield, across
my view, whispers of
"leav-ing, leav-ing, leav-ing."

Car-motion sips of 7-11 coffee,
the lukewarm jolt of java needles
that puncture my steel
blue eyes, awash with his departing.

The stripe in his shirt, the suede
on his Vans, his glass frames
and my drab did-you-pack words
of a crossed-off- yesterday
list. Grey:

walls, carpet,
mattress, desk,
chair, lamp
in his dorm room that shines
silver, in my son's eyes.

Return To School

2. Student of Science

A khaki duffel bag
on her white eyelet spread,
a black bottomed blackness
that stows her belongings.

She laughs as I tell her
I never understood her passion
for calculus, never felt the elation
in a physics equation revealed.

She tosses in: opaque black
leotards, Levi's, tee-shirts, nubbled
grey work socks, well-worn
Birkenstocks.

I tell her, I never needed to classify
rocks as sedimentary
or metamorphic,
they were always just there.

I will her to leave the room
so I can reach inside, pack
silks and lace in colours
of fuscia, lavender and green.

like the pretty-girl-clothes she flung
to the foot of her bed,
that I grouped,
laundered and pressed
while she grew
more like her Dad,
less a biological extension of me.

A rose ribbon dangles
from her lamp. I reach to tie it
to the strap of her bag,
to identify her from the rest,

then refrain. 3000 miles is enough
geography between us.

Mother's Stroke

1. Watching

I watch you
lying shriveled and still
on faded blue hospital sheets. Pale
blue, never a color you wore well.

Small tubes protrude from the grey
vein in your right wrist, drip
strength through you.

I wipe the drooping
side of your mouth
where your words trickle out
in sleepy confusion.

It's hard to watch
you struggle, to speak
a new language
with old words.

I study the soft folds
along your cheek,
around your neck.
When did they appear,

make you look like my grandmother,

your mother,
who lay in a similar bed
a childhood ago

when I watched you
watch her?

Mother's Stroke

2. Listening

Her words will not gather
in crisp orderly rows
but in clotted
clumps of sorrow.

Medicated memories spin,
drop in messy piles
for her to sort
in silence.

Familiar love words
"don't fret, Dear'"
"love you bunches,"
struggle for release, rust

tinted like this Autumn morning
coated with early Winter
frost.

All around her, whitecoats
talk in loud voices,
confuse her muteness
as lack of understanding.

Mother's Stroke

3. Talking

"They left for school,"
>Her watery eyes blink.
>She hears me, always has.

"They're really gone now, aren't they?" I ask
knowing she can't answer,
knowing I know
the answer.

"They're ready, I know they are."

>She nods a slow yes.

"So am I. Lots I want
to do now. So much time
for me."

>She stares past the vertical blinds.

"It's all changing, Mom."

>She opens her lips, a garble of dry
>sound reaches to comfort me.

I see the shift
in her, the distance much greater
than missing
children.

I reach
for the water glass
with the bent straw,
place a towel on her chest,
hold her head
as she sips and spills,

I feel
her fine hair
flattened and knotted.

"Would you like me to brush your hair?
Wash your face?"

Requiem For A Neighbor's Child

1. Young James

From my window,

I watched Jim Adams bury his son today.
He removed his Nikes and jeans
and dressed him in a private

school uniform with a choke
button collar, bristle blue
blazer and oxford lace-up shoes.

He buried him

in forty minute
bus rides and cold
bag lunches. Buried

his six year old tears
in a buck-up boy coffin
quilted with Tuesday

violin lessons, Wednesday
tennis and Thursday
elocution.

Young James, four feet under
September. Under old
boy dreams hanging on little
boy shoulders.

Requiem For A Neighbor's Child

2. Young Anna

She walks through childhood barefoot
on a path of polished glass, fearing
one slip, one tumble, one
errant shard would slow her

almost 'A' average that didn't
win awards. She almost
made the track team but didn't
get invited to Brittany's birthday,
or Ashley's or Cloe's. Didn't
tell her Mother. She tried

to mend her too long skirt
once with sticky tape
because it tripped her,
scabbed and scarred her
bony knees.

From the eighteenth fairway
her parents watch, tally
the cost of her

crystal education, their access
to social elevation
on a path of polished glass.

A Vision of 'Adam' in Safeway

If Adam had picked the apple
would we have crowned him king?

Gusty to grab the moment,
a creator of ribless rules?

Would we judge him

worthy to enter the checkout
counter with the switched off light,

the number two deluminated,
convenience denied to all

but an Adam, worthy to receive
a passing cashier blessing, his debit

payment for new rules set by a man,
who never considered the Safeway queues?

Adam in a hurry

to pay for an autumn bag
of BC apples.

Second Cup Is Free

1. "Second cup, Ma'am?"

I sip my skinny latte and the fat
man across the room fiddles
with gold neckchains, twists
a diamond pinkie ring, flashes
a silvercapped smile

at a Clairol blonde who leaves ruby lips
on a white mug of black coffee. A stream
of nylon leg flows down the length

of her stool, a curl of ankle around
its base. I imagine her combing crimson
Manchu nails through his chest hair, accessing
her needs tangled

with old coffee house memories, of folk
guitars and wild haired boys, unadorned
and naked. "A second cup, Ma'am?"
asks the waitress.

Second Cup Is Free

2. "Refill, Boys?"

The window booth orders
four cups of regular roast, light
their smokes and speak
in the listen-to-me voices
of those seldom asked
their opinions.

Chairman of The Board views
submitted with slow, low words
and nicotine wisdom,
with investments

in rattle coughs, falling ash
and another smoke to puff
up their thoughts, exhale their relief
from Visa bills, taxes,
and rising union dues.

Old agendas about raising kids, the value
of a fifth wheel, their wives'
female complaints and a whisper of poor
Fred's prostate.

"Refill, boys?" the waitress asks.

They pause to stir and sip, then start
the jokes, begun by one voice
finish by another. Jokes
about 'those damn college kids
who never have to start at the bottom,
and aren't married.'

And their own babies
that just came and came
and do you remember
the '28 football team, those noisy
crinolines and itchy angora sweaters!

They laugh.

I finish my latte, pass
on a refill. Wonder
if my son passed his algebra exam.

Dear Quebec,

Where do we file our memories
after you vote them away?
The 'un petit, deux petits, trois
Canadiens' who learned to pay
taxes in two languages.

Where do we store Miss Saunder's salt-
clay models? Fifth grade projects
of ribbon strip seigneuries, flat-top
homes spaced along the blue
tempera painted St. Laurence.

And where do we house Paul,
Catherine, Monsieur
and Madame Thibault?
Textbook friends who challenged
our vowels with stretch of tongue
and tone, as we chatted

and walked Pitou
down the Champs D'Elysee
which we wished was our St Catherine's
and promised to visit after
Quebec City, after a carriage ride
from the Chateau Frontenac, "with a view
of the Plains of Abraham, please,"
remembering the English
General pickled in rum, transported
to a Westminster tomb.

Where do we record Les Coureur de Bois,
La Verendrye and LaValle? Lament
Oh Canada, over dreams of youth fearful
to study at McGill. With faith
we immersed them in French
skills, to better understand and still
they ask us Why? When? How

could you let...? as we quietly file away
the Who in the morning news. Baffled

by this man who never ventured outside
'his' province until mid-life. His crisis
a swap of sport car dreams
for a visionary crown. His kingdom carved
from the heart
of our country, our history,
our children's heritage.

Hands: Reflections On Swiss Air Flight 411

1.

Salt-callused hands sift
through familiar nets, filled
with catches
of a newly seeded sea.

Hand over hand over heart

they reach into the tangle,
remove remnants
of metal, fabric and bone
entwined with domestic stocks.

Dread of the catch,
of the day. And evening
prayers of release are all
that is left to gather.

Soon media crews will leave.
Families will try to say good-bye.

Fishernets will be mended
again and again
and tossed into the deep.

2.

On a rescue boat's crusty deck,
a sodden stuffed bear,
a reminder
of damp doughy hands,
pudding fingers

a soother thumb,
or fingerclump
in a drizzling mouth.

Did his mother hold
the oxygen mask firm, cradle
damp curls to her breast, breathe
a last whiff of Ivory scrub,

hum a lullaby?

3.

They hold hands, jam two sets
of arthritic knuckles together. Two
worn gold bands etch new lines
between flesh and bone.

Forty years together.
Silence.

4.

A gash in a September morning. Liverspotted, cropped-nailed hands pour
comfort into Styrofoam cups. Sugar-laced tea from thermoses, butter slices
of homebaked bread. 'A full stomach, a brave heart.' Women's hands used
to mending.

5.

Empty eyes
scan endless grey
for a miracle, a mistake.

With open palms
ready
to reach, to hold
one more
opportunity,

filled instead
with one more
damp tissue.

Wind burnt fingers
too numb to hold
a cup of sugared tea.

6.

World of hands,
raise tents
of prayer
pointing

to six minutes
that hold us
still.

In From The Cold ❧

"And love is a cord woven out of life,
And died in the red of the living heart;
And time is the hunter's rusty knife,
That cannot cut the red strands apart."

Isabella Valancy Crawford
(*The Camp of Souls*)

"These are the days that try us; these the hours
That find us, or leave us, cowards"

Susie Francis Harrison
(*November*)

Under The Doorframe

She waits in the open doorway, under
the white aluminum doorframe. She could go

outside, get in the car and drive
away and away and anywhere

away from his disappointment.
She could step back around the corner

to where he kissed her, told her he was glad
there was only them. Glad of two

incomes, their plans and her good sense.
The space before

the blue dot on the drugstore test
and the gold wedding bands

that bound them to work it out.
Still her secret, a frightened shiver inside.

Outside snow falls slowly
one random flake at a time.

Under the doorframe, neither here
nor there, she waits.

A Woman's Place

Winter mornings, 2:00 a.m., I rose
in the deep breath silence, retrieved

my trousseau blue Samsonite, and flew
British Airways direct to London, where

a black helmet cab deposited me
at Number 46 Earls Court Road, at a small flat

willed by some old Aunt, who thought
a woman should have secrets

a place to escape and fill
with market tulips, chintz and red wine.

I would sink into a plump feather bed,
pull a victory garden quilt up

to my chin and wait for a peek
of English morning through lace curtains,

wait for the first scent of breakfast
sausages and browning toast, wait for cries

of my hungry babies needing
another bottle, another change,

another day.

In From The Cold

I'm first in the door, first
to feel the batten warmth
on my cheeks, iced
from tobogganing
on Christ Church hill.
First

to drop a puddle of damp mitts,
scarf and toque on the tile,
unzip my jacket, kick
my boots to the corner
and sprint to heat

milk, add scoops
and scoops of Nestle's Quick,
pour warmth into four
waiting mugs. Mine the blue
china mug I dropped

into my school bag, that day
my Grandmother died. The blue
china mug with the chipped rim
like a tooth to avoid,
a one-sided smile.

I only took the mug, not her silver
brushes or her quill pens or sepia photos.
Only what her lips had touched.

Her words and mine
melded together on winter afternoons
in a bond of real
cocoa, sugar and cream.

I sip the hot chocolate, feel
porcelain heat my fingers, hear myself speak,
"So what was the best part of your day?"
My Grandmother's words. I listen

to the list of snow, bumps,
tumbles, bruises, cold, sip
slowly, savour.

Sunday Night Calls

1. Answering Machine

Again, I listen to my son's words, captive
in the answering machine.
Between the clearing, rinsing
and washing-up I listen
to his timbre, his cadence.

I try to decode the amount
of green vegetables in his diet,
Crest on his breath, scent of Tide
in his shirt and length of his hair.

"Could you advance me fifty dollars?" I sense
the rush. "Thanks, speak to you soon."
A mingle of his high and some low
female voice that whispers him away.

The hasty "Bye Mom"
that encases me.
I press the repeat button
again.

Sunday Night Calls

2. Do I Tell Her?

Do I tell her he is only the first, the one
she will remember, when her daughter is in love?

> That his spearmint kisses won't last,
> but her Chem marks will,
> and Grad School won't care
> that his eyes are watered jade.

Do I tell her that his arms haven't yet grown
enough muscle to hold her?

> She tells me, Plato's 'Republic' makes sense,
> when he explains it and she better understands
> Elizabeth's sacrifice of Lord Dudley.

Do I tell her to leave
a small window, open to breath?

> She tells me, when he holds her
> she doesn't feel the chill
> off Lake Ontario and has stopped yearning
> for the Rockies.

Our Sunday night calls have changed. We talk briefly
of papers, exams and labs. She experiments
with a trust that tests my silence.

Sunday Night Calls

3. What's New

I don't want to be the problem,
the grit I hear in their voices
Sunday nights, when I ask
"What's new? "

I want to celebrate
their changes, admit I haven't
yet. I still want
the role of Mother, confidante,
fixer of the scrapes

they want to solve
to solve themselves. Want
to apply their own salve
or one provided by others.
Want to fall, even welcome
the pain.

Call it theirs. Call it not mine.

So I try new strategies.
Keep myself busy being
busy, bend and twist
in new positions.

Show them I can be flexible.
Sometimes
wish they could re-flex
to the old ways, wonder

how long it will take
for me to become
what's new.

Care Package

Packed in a 4 litre Tupperware container:
one new white tee, two pair
cotton panties coiled around six
florescent pencils with turquoise erasers,

> to smudge the sharp
> questions she didn't want
> to hear, that the Mother
> in me needed to ask.
> A recipe

for six alarm chili, three
double fudge chocolate bars,
a gift certificate to Second Cup
and a new blue toothbrush

> to brush away the taste
> of words we never meant
> to use, never have used
> before. A black

tube of mascara, two
bubble bath samples and a jar
of Cherry lip balm

> to put a smile back on her lips
> when she thinks of the foolish
> contents of this package.
> A red rimmed

lid snaps all in place.
I wrap it carefully
in kraft paper

> the color of truce
> reaching across Canada, reaching
> to touch her.

Christmas Break

1. Changing Linens

I ready my son's room
for his return. Change
the linens I couldn't change
when he left, last Fall.

Because the scent of him
was more than jogging
and Scotch could replace.
His blend

of Head and Shoulders,
rugby game smells
on his skin, his action
dreams, girl dreams,

the peaty night sweats
that Monday morning
always washed away.

I spread fresh sheets taut,
tuck hospital corners, recall
his baritone

"Just about ready Mom.
Only a Stats exam left.
I'll catch the 5:15 bus.
Oh, and did I tell you I grew
a beard again?"

I picture blonde whiskers
on his cheeks, his chin, his barbs
of manhood that shy me,
Nature's fence that reminds me,

we must stand well apart
for him to be a man.

I tug striped cases over pillows,
fluff them high and full, pull
the quilt up to where his chin should be.
My lips leave a dent on the pillow.

Christmas Break

2. Cranberry Pancakes

I haven't held her for four months. Haven't
felt her fluff fine hair, in the cup of my hand,
the 20 year old softness of her cheeks
But tomorrow I will

smell the sweet musk of my lavender
scented sheets on her skin, warm
from a mulled sleep, in her childhood
bed. Tomorrow

I'll make cranberry pancakes and nod yes
to her maple syrup request. She will sit
on the kitchen stool in the blue bunny robe
she left behind and we will talk

of ooids and oolids and other geological terms
that form the new language of her. And I
will listen hard, ask questions, learn all
that is important. Try to hold

the image of her firm enough
to brace my January days
and beyond.

English Trifle #1
January 1975

A Bridal Shower Gift
Enshrined in Plastic

From: She who has raised perfection
To: She who does not feel worthy

Prepare cake three days in advance. use only the freshest ingredients.
Place cakes in a cool dry environment, uncovered.

> Survey day-old pound cakes, a Safeway's brand
> pushed to the back of the counter, away
> from the cat. Drying nicely, firm yet not crumbly.

Homemade raspberry jam: fresh freezer jam would do.

> Smuckers will have to.

Custard: use the freshest of eggs to achieve the creamiest results.

> Bird's Eye container winks
> with Crayola colored simplicity,
> a conspirator in the fraud.

Sherry or grape juice

> 2 royal blue bottles of Harvey's Bristol Cream
> stand at military precision, to serve, to protect
> this revered legacy.

Raspberries - fresh

> From my freezer. Del Monte joins the clan.

Whipping cream - optional

> So is breathing.

Arrange one half of cake, cut into one inch squares, on bottom of clear glass trifle bowl. (My own Mother's favorite bowl, brought with her to Canada as a reminder of the necessity to maintain civilized Sunday dinners.)

47

My bread knife leaves random size refugees
spread in abandonment over the terrain.
Helping hands transport them to a safe haven.
Some are missing in action.

Pour half of sherry mixture over cubes

Not before it undergoes quality testing
to make sure it is worthy.

Add raspberries, being careful not to bruise, squeeze,

batter, mutilate, pulverize, disembowel.
Enough sherry!
REMINDER: This is to be 'the crowning glory'
to Sunday dinner.

Over a mixture add one half of cool custard

fresh from the microwave.

Now girl: Whip that cream.
Pour that custard.
Repeat those layers.
Top with cream.
Chill until cold.

And most important

Please the Mother-in-law.

English Trifle #2
January 1999

I found the flour sifter in your cupboard.
Upper left shelf, behind the tin canisters.
I sifted the ingredients carefully.
Into the whiteness, I broke the yellow
yolks - the color of old fears - I wasn't
afraid. The whites were beaten
separately, by hand then folded like lace
hankies into a soapy wash basin.

It baked. I sat. For three days
watched it age and shrivel.
Last summer we picked the raspberries
from your canes and froze them
ruby and ripe. Pricked my fingers
many times and used language
you wouldn't.

The custard is still Bird's Eye.
How we would argue and laugh
as we both acknowledged its texture
and flavor. I haven't your patience
for perfection.

I will assemble the layers later today,
using our bowl, taking pleasure
in the placement of each uniform square
of cake—each bite an equal measure, a fair
taste of life—I'll carefully place each berry
in thanksgiving.

I will use the non-alcoholic Sherry, respecting
your medication, but I will toast you
with the real. I don't need its false courage,
just its time flavored memory.

Tonight, after the roast beef and Yorkshire
pudding, I will serve you the English Trifle.
Like the lady you are, you will taste
and quietly acknowledge its flavor,
neither judging nor commenting, oblivious
to the labored details of this world.
You won't remember. It doesn't matter.
I have enough memories for us both.

January

A grey winter snow
covers warmth
buries her
color.

A reflection
in a frozen sunlit pool.
Two faces cast back:

her mother's glassy stare,
her daughter's distant
gaze.

She rolls over,
pulls the layered quilt
to her face and fades
into a dream
of Spring.

Onions

Across the cafe table, Grace utters old
woman words, "You shouldn't order
the onions. You know you'll suffer." Burning

words disguised as love.
Married words of years
of ignoring the man
behind

the drooping left lip,
food stained tie,
shallow sloping shoulders,
who once promised he would carry

all her hurts and never forget
her name.

Night Storm on The Georgia Straits

1.

A fresh race of wind
through the still
dark cedars. Hushed morning
whispers turn

to orders: a neighbour's flag snaps taut,
lawnchairs fall flat,
a brass windchime
once a gentle tumble of notes,
now a clash and wail.

I rise from bed, watch spits
of rain hit the window like careless
highway pebbles tossed
against a windshield.

A silver glint off the swell
of waves, the spew
of angry sky.
Morning crashes open.

2.

No stars. No moon. Nothing to reflect
the night. A defiant tugboat
huddles against the shore,
along the Robert's Creek coast, seeks
any smudge of yellow light.

Its silhouette in banners
of red and white lights, that tilt
across its bow. Engine's steady
'ohm', a chant, a prayer
to Saint Christopher.

In workhorse manner
it plods the night, waits
for an open gate to amble
its whipping log boom down,
down and steady down
the Georgia Straits
to the safety of Port Mellon.

3.

This winter storm,
like edgy hormones, a misery
to all, like a petulant child looking
for attention, like unsettled differences,
calms by midmorning, leaves

puddles of last nights fury,
pouts of grey sky,
and no real damage.

How simple the rage.
How simple the morning.

A Melt of Snow ⊗

"There is a transparency to life –
and mystery – and light projects
a new assurance as it fills
the day"

Lewis Horne
("Watching My Daughters Drive Off For University")

Chinook

Did you taste the wind today,
as it swept the Elbow Valley clean
of snow and chunks of chill?
Did it tempt your tongue with flavours
of soil, root and green?

Did you hear a rattle at your window
as it rode the morning streets
with stampede fury, toppling
lids off garbage tins, whipping
the Glenmore Reservoir into icy froth?

And through a west window, did you watch

a band of blue marry mountains
with morning sky, pledge hot
gusty vows, as the mountain
ash danced and danced in celebration,
shaking old winter berries
to the ground?

Did it lift your heels
and dance you down the street,
make you want to fling your coat
and follow it anywhere,
anywhere to stretch
the moment?

Spring Training

Today we feel like girls
Diane, Deborah and I,
reckless and trusting

> our feet to the slip and gasp
> of last patches of black ice
> hidden under sidewalk snow. Still careful

not to 'step on cracks, break
our mother's backs' or hips
or femurs. We giggle, link arms

> walk in stride, in new
> Nikes that pinch
> our resolve to combat

the leaving of cycles
we once cursed. Leaving us,
one at a time,

> with rebel bones, raw
> emotions and freckles
> that grow, turn

to spots and lumps
that always need checking.
We side step down the hill,

> smell the wandering
> dogs that roamed before us,
> taste morning chill, the growing

warmth on our backs
and the green, the new green
we have seen before,

but never like this. Today
we feel like Spring,
our birthing work done,

returning home
trusting our feet
to familiar paths.

We pause, tighten our laces
and embrace our growing
forward together.

Kittens

An apple box in Anna's closet
cradles four kittens, born yesterday,
looking like their prey, tiny
as emaciated mice.

Two grey, two black and dark.

Their eyes not open,
ears not released, they follow smells
of mothercat moving in the rose
and blue flannel cocoon.

If I reach inside, cup one
warm body in my hand, feel
the damp, the wiggle,
the squirm.

If I squeeze tight
and tighter and tightest,
a minor struggle,
a smothered mew,
then nothing

but animal shame, a black
stain forever
on the rose and blue
in my life.

Kittens, too grey, too black and dark.

Spring Thaw

1. White Lies

She'll not be home,
for Spring Break but will lie
on a Florida beach, with him.
"Mom I need sun, not cold,"
she will lie. And I

will send her a gift,
a little lie of snow
white terry towel, a gown
to wear to and from the sand,
to dry her chin to toe
as she steps from the Atlantic.

I will lie.
Say it doesn't matter,
say I understand her change
of plans and she will phone me

next week, tell me
it was wonderful, tell me
she missed me.

Spring Thaw

2. How Far To Florida?

As far as a thumb to pinkie trip
on page 42 of the Rand McNally.
As far as gunshot sounds

from my TV. The random shootings
and interstate accidents, crime
rates and Canadian license plates. Farther
than Mounties can patrol the shots
that drive through my mind.

Florida seems farther than this
sheet of paper I am trying to fill
with a pointless pencil.

How far to Florida?
As far as Jupiter, farther
than Mars, than sunscreen
can safely cover and VISA cards
and medical insurance can protect.

Farther than Christmas to May,
Sunday to Saturday. As far
as 2:00 a.m. is to sanity.
My list

of closets to organize,
windows to wash,
drawers to clean, jottings
of scour, scrub and sort.
as far as the trip that ends
when she phones.

"Hey, Mom, how was your week?"

"Busy," I'll reply and that's as far
as I will go.

Spring Thaw

3. A Day Off

I tried on red spike heels at Brown's.
Felt like Barbie, grown up, a little
blowzy. Then sampled

makeup at the Bay, chose Sapphire
Sun over Sultana Raisin, felt
scented and expensive, like my new lips
wrapped in a box, cellophane,
tissue and bow. Felt ready

for lunch at Moxies.
"Will anyone be joining you?
"No," I said watching a young mother
calming her infants rattle angry
cry. 'No,' I said, as she left
and I stayed and wasn't even tempted

by the veggie stir fry, ordered
"A BLT with extra B please
and coffee, double cream, no froth."
Stayed for a second cup. Didn't stop

for groceries, moved on to Birks.
Studied diamonds, emeralds and pearls
left them in an unsuitable heap, then settled

in my car to drive home. Waited
in the parking lot to listen to the end

of a radio interview.
A mother in Saskatoon
telling her story,
the crisis on her family farm. I listened

to her dreams
for her children to leave,
create lives away
from home, away
from droughts, rising taxes and falling
grain prices.

I listened to her day off.

Spring Thaw

4.She Fades

She fades a little
with every "Thanks
for the care package.
Mom, sorry I can't chat."

She is buried under layers
of final exams, lab reports
and school forms. She fades

like my overwashed apron
terminally stained with baby
peas, spaghetti sauce, gravy
and chocolate.

She hasn't shared the late
March snow that split the weeping
birch, hasn't tasted the whiff
of soil in the air. She hasn't
seen the ash

tones in my hair or how
'Sapphire Sun' stains a smile
on my lips. She fades
to paler shades than the peach
roses I brought home. Sunday

she phoned. Told me she wants
a summer job in Kingston. And I faded
into old patterns. Felt a new
voice inside me grow,
"Go for it," I said.
It's time.

A Melt of Snow

I remember red roses gathered
one lover at a time. Always felt
for the barbs. Seldom found
until color faded. I collected them
never caring if they were taken
from some garden or hot house.
I remember

fingers entwined with mine;
the roughness of the ranch hand,
softness of the account agent,
sweat firm hold of the rugby player.
I remember

their kisses heated to a bruise,
ridges on my inner lip a callus blue

and words spoken with deep breath promise,
laughing revelations.
When one day without conversation
was an endurance, two an eternity,
until polite words were all
that were left. I remember

all of them: the Brute, the Old Spice,
the deodorant mingled
with my Chanel. All stale now.
Until a warm spring breeze rouses
a melt of snow.

The Reflecting Pool

Today, she rises, climbs back up
Mount Helion to the pool, where
once Narcissus enticed her to lie
on the bank and gaze at the surface.

"Reflect on yourself,' he said.
"All knowledge lies in this transparent face."

Today winds ripple the calm.
Her reflection is tangled among grey
weeds. Gone the gleaming
curls of a fragile girl.

Today she rises,
brushes away the fragile
petals white and ponders where
she can find a glorious gown
of dusty rose.

I've Never Been To Winnipeg

I've never been to Winnipeg, but I've visited
Portage and Main. Felt the scald of sun on bare
shoulders, dust-peppered by winds
propelling me on. I've felt the sting
of snow strike my face, weave through thin
wool gloves and clutch
my fingers with squeezing
cold.

I've sat on the banks of the Red
River, thought of Red River carts
like the one at the Glenbow. I studied
the raw-hide tethered wheels
supporting the basket frame, transporting
fragile dreams over tough
prairie.

I've never been to Winnipeg
but I've stood in the centre of Canada
among people not needing
to label it
central.

I've never been to Winnipeg, but I've walked
its streets teeming with people seeking
refuge from nature. I've sat by a motel
swimming pool, listened to a woman mourn
the dairy cattle she slaughtered,
so they would not drown, and her four
year old son sheltered from it all
dives off the edge.

I've poured coffee in soup kitchens
and contemplated the grey
pebble-faced man from Ste. Agathe
describing his loss:
his home, his dog, his belief
in God's will.

I've never been to Winnipeg
but I've waded deep into a soggy field,
watched construction crews
scoop loamy topsoil, transport it north
to build dikes. I've dried tears
from a lined face recounting the years

of nurturing the rich growing soil,
his Grandfather's work, his father's
work, his work washing downstream
to nowhere. Never again
to grow crops to feed his family.

I've never been to Winnipeg but I watched
our Prime Minister place a sandbag on a wall.
His people asking him to value them,
postpone his coronation, remember
who he works for. I've listened as he tells
them to file their tax returns
a little later, when they're not stressed.

I've never been to Winnipeg
but lately I can't seem to be
anywhere else.

Who Is Elise?

Adam's mother who
packed his green
college trunks, wept
for months. She mailed
her caring in packages,
with knots tied tight.
Mourning faded and she unwound

one day, stepped out
of loafers, slipped
on sandals with tinkle-toe rings
and ankle straps, zipper gowns
of lace and chintz flowing
from her shoulders, swirling
about her shins. She drifted.

Sold her stocks. Her future
investments, paid cash
for groceries at Rimbley's
Market, delighting
in the leaf crisp crackle
of bills piled beside kumquats,
asparagus, shrimp and coconut milk,

packed loosely into India bags
with circle mirrors stitched
to the sides, reflecting
those on the outside.

A Winter Journal

She rises at five to write
in a drugstore journal
with her Father's Parker pen, staining
white pages with blue battles
caught and tossed between
night and dawn.

She writes in darkness
Her fingers guiding blind
words to invisible
lines, cold to touch,
her palm blots sharp thoughts
blurs the tone before
the ochre and rose

of morning sun rises
on her reflections of why
she needs this time
to be alone.

Avignon Fields

Unbound, her auburn hair brushed
a waist thickened by distant
childbirth scents, replaced
with lavender picked
that summer in Avignon fields.

Where sunflowers followed
and begged she pluck them,
twine them tight about her
mane and race with her
through vineyards ripe
with abandon. At night

she drinks Bordeux. Sleeps ruby
with tomorrow's plans, forgotten
in a Matisse sun until October,
when she turned

west, recalled the still
white of her Rockies, mailed postcards
to her son reading 'soon.' Promised
when snow crept through
her strands, she would return.

Amber Beads

She wears a strand of amber
beads with needles trapped
inside. Time frozen in toffee
from trees formed three million years
before. Elise

carries a Constantine coin
in her left pocket, one month's pay
to a Roman Centurion
far from home in 200 AD, bought
at The British Museum
for twelve pounds.

She eats bleached bread
and black olives with cheddar
cheese ages forte and strong,
wonders if there's time
for a tawny port at The Whistle
before the BBC news, before

Adam's weekly call
and the rugby pictures and the letters
on the dresser, that developed voice
and again query when
she is coming home.

Quotes ❧

Anne Wilkinson, In June And Gentle Oven, 1955, pg 60
Poetry By Canadian Women, Edited by Rosemary Sullivan,
Toronto, Oxford University Press, 1989.

Lorna Crozier, Late Afternoon, Pg 69,
A Saving Grace, McClelland and Stewart Inc., 1996.

Isabella Valancy Crawford, The Camp of Souls, pg 10,
Poetry By Canadian Women (see above)

Susie Frances Harrison, November, 189
Poetry By Canadian Women (see above)

Lewis Horne, Watching My Daughters Drive Off For University, Pg
109, In The Clear, A Contemporary Canadian Poetry Anthology,
Thistledown Press Ltd., 1998